History Of Ice Harvesting Days In The Late 18th And Early 19th Century

"And Stories from The Older folks"

History of Ice Harvesting Days In the Late 18th And Early 19th Century "And Stories from the Older Folks"

© 2004 J. Samuel King. All rights reserved. No portion of this book may be reproduced, stored in a retrieval system, or transmitted in any form or by any other means—electronic, mechanical, photocopy, recording, or any other—except for brief quotations in printed reviews, without the prior written permission of the publisher.

Cover art by Sylvia Ann Fisher.

Printed at
Masthof Press
219 Mill Road
Morgantown, PA 19543-9516

Dedication

After purchasing some ice equipment, I started asking the older folks about harvesting ice in Lancaster County. Most I spoke with provided hearsay information, although if they were age 90 or older, they recalled some. There is still ice harvesting in some areas today, but not in Lancaster County. After Grandpa had a light stroke, I started writing his stories. He told me these stories many times over the years.

Interestingly, when a horse hitched to a spring wagon goes down the road it used to haul feed for the cattle. Today, instead of feed it carries bulk foods and snacks. In the late 18th and early 19th century, people primarily were connected to agriculture.

This book is the result of many conversations and contacts made with local historical societies.

I have not written this book because of any connection to relations or friends, but to share some stories. Hopefully, the readers will enjoy it and God bless.

Contents

Preface vii

Part I. Icehouses and Cold Storage Houses 1

Part II. Ice Harvesting 18

Part III. Great-Grandfather 33

Part IV. The Beacon Light 51

Part V. Bake Oven 54

Part VI. Grandma and Grandpa 56

PREFACE

After seeing ice equipment advertised on a sale bill in January 2003, I asked my Grandpa, "What is ice equipment?"

He replied, "Well, when I was about nine years old, my Dad sold our ice equipment to a farmer who lived three miles from our place. All I know is it had two handle bars like a garden harrow. If you go to that sale, I would like to go along."

The sale date soon arrived, but it was too cold to take Grandpa along. But when I was milking the cows that morning, my Dad came to the barn and asked if I'm going to the sale.

I said, "Well, I'll see yet. I'm not sure!" Then Dad said, "I'd like to have that ice equipment."

"Well, I'll go see what it looks like," I replied.

When I got there, the ice equipment was in the front yard. At least I thought that was what it was. I had no idea how it looked like, but when I saw the ice cutter that you hitch a horse in, I knew it had to be the one. And the hand saw included two ice tongs. I purchased it and brought it home.

That evening I said to Grandpa, "Look what I have in my barn." He looked at it for awhile, and said, "That's the one! I didn't see it for eighty years."

I also purchased, a few of Grandpa's favorite stories: *The Beacon Light; Driving Cattle on the Road*. This book is based on true facts.

PART I

ICEHOUSES AND COLD STORAGE HOUSES

By *Professor R. P. Clarkson*
From Farm Knowledge *Sears Roebuck Co.*, *1918*

    Aside from the advantages it offers as a means for keeping foods of all kinds in good condition in hot weather, there are two reasons why every farmer should cut and save his own supply of ice. In the first place, it can be done at no cost except that of labor and hauling expense. Secondly, the work is done during the winter months when no other jobs demand immediate attention. Moreover, there is always a market for any surplus, either in the nearest village or among neighbors.

    The use of canned goods and the tendency to buy meats the butcher rather than to raise, kill, and dress them, have to some extent dimmed the importance of cold storage facilities. But to balance this, the increasing popularity and use of concrete and hollow tile offer the inducement that an efficient icehouse can be more easily and more inexpensively built, and a supply of ice more easily gathered and more economically kept than ever before. Every farmer within reach of a pond and freezing weather should learn it, use it, and profit by it.

    For more than 100 years, traffic in ice has been carried on until it has so outgrown natural supplies that artificial ice can be sold in most sections cheaper than natural ice. Since about 1830 when the export trade reached its height, practically all tropical supplies have been produced artificially on the spot; whereas before that time thousands of tons of ice were shipped around the world. Notwithstanding this situation, the individual farm icehouse stored up the natural ice from some small nearby pond. The lack of a natural pond or of a freezing climate does not, by any means, shut him off from the advantages of cold storage. Artificial-ice plants, refrigerating methods without ice, and other methods of preservation, are all open to him at comparatively small cost.

Icehouses for the farm. The advantage and convenience of having a good supply of ice goes far beyond the small cost of gathering it; not only for the general farmer, but also for the dairyman, the country merchant, and the rural dweller. Often a vacant shed, a corner of the barn, unused cellar, an empty silo, a vegetable storehouse, a dry well, or even an old cistern in the ground, when properly cleansed and fitted up in accordance with the principles here given, will serve as a satisfactory icehouse for many years.

The successful icehouse is not necessarily the most expensive one. In southern Virginia, a hole dug in the ground entirely above the water level and lined with native clay held ice satisfactorily through the fall. Its' only covering was of leaves and pine boughs. This was the type used by the Romans in the early ages to preserve snow, and it is now quite common in many parts of the country.

As another extreme of simple construction, a farmer in New York built four walls of a single thickness of board supported by upright green poles freshly cut from the woods. He filled it with ice surrounded by a foot of sawdust, a layer of sawdust for the floor, and another layer for covering. It had no roof, doors, nor windows, and the ice kept all summer without much waste. This type is not suggested for the natural-ice dealers.

Secret of keeping ice. It is obvious from these two examples that building material, whether wood, earth, stone, brick, or concrete, may not be the deciding factor in the keeping of ice. The secret is in the strict observance of four principles all of which finally reduce to one, namely, good insulation.

First, there must be good under-drainage to carry off the melted ice; otherwise it would form a conductor of heat to the remainder of the stored ice, and would gradually melt it from underneath. Water melts ice much faster than air, for the latter merely affects the surface while the former penetrates throughout.

Second, there must be perfect ventilation at the top of the ice in order that the covering of sawdust, straw, hay moss, or leaves, may be kept as dry as possible so that it will not form a conductor for the heat from the air and melt the ice on top.

Third, the ice must be packed so as to prevent the circulation of air through the mass, because heated air will certainly enter into the house when the doors, windows, ventilators, or top are opened. These currents of air rapidly warm up, while dead air does not readily become heated because air is a poor conductor of heat.

Fourth, good insulation at the sides and bottom must be carefully provided.

Size and capacity of house. The size of the house may be determined from the fact that a ton of stored ice occupies approximately 42 cubic feet of space. The average size of house for a small farm is about 10 feet high from the ground to eaves, with an inside area of 12x14 feet. After allowing for the space occupied by the sawdust around and under the ice, this will provide for storage of from 25 to 28 tons of ice.

A cubic foot of solid ice weighs close to $57\frac{1}{4}$ pounds, so that 35 cubic feet of ice would weigh a ton. From this, we can estimate the amount possible to cut from a pond. The thickness of the cakes usually range from six inches in the central states to 16 and even 20 inches in the north; probably 12 to 14 inches is the average. The cakes are cut in various sizes, also; perhaps 12x16 and 16x16 are common sizes, but this is not important. Assuming cakes are 12 inches thick and 12x16 inches, there will be 26 of them to a ton, each one weighing 76 1/3 pounds. In the field, allowing for breakage and waste, a surface of 50 square feet will harvest at least 45, and possibly 50, tons of 12 inch ice.

Care of the ice field. The essential thing is to provide for clear clean ice of sufficient thickness. Before the water freezes, it must be purified as much as possible. Sources of possible pollution must be removed, all rubbish taken away from the field and branches or floating logs cleared out. These carefully observed will insure clean ice. Motion of the water during freezing not only expels the air but also promotes the growth in thickness. By expelling the air, the ice is made clear. Sometimes it is desirable to induce a gentle current through the field during ice-making weather for this purpose, as well as to obtain the additional thickness. The method of doing this in the case of landlocked ponds is to provide an outlet which must be readily controlled, because a too rapid or violent motion will retard the growth of ice.

After freezing has taken place, the watchfulness of the farmer is properly directed towards increasing the thickness of the ice and keeping it clean. The handling of snow is important. Except in warm weather, snow should be removed as soon as possible, since it prevents the escape of heat from the water and thus retards growth of the ice. In soft weather, however, the snow is desirable to act as a blanket in shielding the water and ice from the heat of the sun. The heat of rain is largely used in melting the snow and thus does not affect the ice too much.

Clearing off snow. After a thaw, the snow and water on top of the ice freeze and form a porous cloudy layer. If not too thick and it is near the cutting time, this layer is not altogether a detriment. It does detract from the quality of the ice, to be sure, but it makes the handling of the ice easier. It also prevents breakage of cakes in packing either for storage or in shipment.

There are two methods to remove snow. If the ice is strong enough, horse-drawn scrappers are used. If the ice is thin, holes are cut in the ice at every eight or ten feet through which water rises and floods off the snow by melting. Then, as the ice thickens, the snow ice which may be formed is planed off if necessary.

Tapping the ice. Continued soft weather or a thaw during the growth of the ice is one of the serious times with an ice field. If water washes on the ice, it must be removed at once. Usually the only way possible is to tap holes in a number of places so that the water will flow off and the ice, being lighter, will raise. It is not worth doing this if only an inch or two of water stands on top, as this could freeze and may then be planed off.

Harvesting the ice. The first move is to inspect the field thoroughly and mark all shallow or dangerous places. The field is then laid out with a marker, which is really a hand plow made to cut a light groove along the line. The horse plow is set in the groove and run back and forth until the ice is cut more than half through. This is done with all lines in one direction and then with all lines in the other; the pond is thus cut into squares.

The next move is to open a channel by deeply plowing the groove on either side and completely sawing through with an ice saw. This channel section is then split into cakes which are usually pushed under the remaining ice in large ponds to quickly open up the field. In small ponds, however, they may be floated to shore and stored.

With an open channel to shore, sections of perhaps 100 squares are sawed off and floated. These sections are split into cakes just before being pulled out of the water. The

floats, however, must not be left too long, as the grooves will flood and freeze.
Tools required. A field planer, ice auger, tapping axe, snow scraper, marker, horse plow, ice saw, breaking bar, splitting chisel, ice hooks, trimmer bar, ice adze, several grapples, loading tongs, and packing chisel constitute a reasonably full and quite inexpensive equipment for the proper handling of any considerable quantity of ice. For a very small field, it is possible to do without most of these tools. Hoes and scoops or shovels may be substituted for the planer and scraper. A hand marker and an ice saw will cut the field. A pair of tongs will lift each cake out and carry it to the drag or the incline leading to the house and an ordinary axe will trim the cakes. Use of the tools mentioned above save time and labor, especially the former, which is of real importance in harvesting during uncertain weather.

BUILDING THE ICE HOUSE

Material of building. Having determined the size of house and the outlay of money that can be afforded, one must determine the material to be used and the plan to be followed. Beyond any reasonable doubt, wood is better in many ways than stone, brick, or concrete for icehouse construction, although any of these may be used with satisfaction if the ice is packed far from the walls and well insulated with 10 or 12 inches of sawdust. The only objection to wood is its tendency to rot under the continued influence of moisture inside and the dryness outside. For this reason, cypress is highly recommended, although pine will last for some years and is generally used.
Underdrainage and foundation. For a foundation, concrete is best. Let it go into the ground below the frost line and extend a foot above ground, to keep the sills dry. Unless the soil is well drained, there should be a main ditch with side

branches cut in the floor, covering the whole space below the ice, with the main ditch leading out on the lower side. Fill the ditches with broken stone, crockery, brick, or clinkers, and spread a thin layer over the whole floor. On top of the stone, place a layer of straw covered with a thickness of coal ashes. On top of the ashes, place floor boards with cracks between them to allow free drainage of water from the melting ice. More often, however, the boards are dispensed with and an eight- or ten-inch layer of sawdust placed directly on the ashes, and the ice being packed on that.

Side walls and insulation. The walls may be either single or double, and should be built with matched boards or papered with tarred roofing paper. I would recommend both. The paper is cheap, costing $4.50 to $5.00 for a 500-foot roll, and it certainly provides a much better house. If the single walls are papered the papering should be on the outside, of course; but the building is constructed with double walls, the papering should be on the sides within the air space. Double walls are much better for insulation, and may easily be made by nailing the boards on both sides of the 2x4 joists used as uprights. This leaves a four-inch dead air space between the walls, which should not be filled with sawdust nor with anything else.

The best insulator is dead air, and the purpose of the sawdust, felt, wool, shavings, and such substances is merely to keep the air dead—that is, these substances prevent circulation of air by catching small quantities in the spaces between the particles. The use of these substances is not to be recommended, either in icehouses between walls or in the walls of cold-storage boxes.

In either case, the filling would become damp and remain so, thus rotting the construction from the inside. In cold-storage boxes, it will also absorb and retain odors, making the box unfit for holding eatable produce. Furthermore, when damp, such fillings are reasonably good heat conductors.

"**Pocketing" the air.** In the air space between the boards in the icehouse construction, every three or four feet up, there should be a strip of tarred paper tacked, to form a horizontal partition. Thus prevents any up and down circulation of the air. The result of this construction is that the ice is surrounded by walls consisting of a large number of boxes containing dead air. These boxes will be from three to four feet square and four inches thick—the thickness of the air space.

House sills. The sills of the house should be laid directly on the concrete foundation in close union with the concrete, to prevent any entrance of air between them. In my experience, it is desirable to lay a coating of tar or asphalt on the foundation walls and on this put the sills, thus producing an air-tight job. There must be no entrance for air underneath the ice. It is true that a small amount will enter through the drain if the latter is not trapped, but this is not sufficient to do any harm. In a commercial icehouse of large ice, however; the drain should be of tile and trapped as it comes from under the icehouse. Preferably, there is also a drain around the foundation on the outside, with both of the drains brought together and led away to a lower level.

Roof and ventilation. The roof for a small building may be of almost any material to shed the rain, keep off the sun, and provide good ventilation. The latter feature is the most important one in connection with building the house. The ventilators should be closable and kept closed on foggy days and nights. For this reason, trap-doors on the sides and roof are preferable.

The roof should be a V-shaped or hipped roof, with trap-doors at each end and at the ridge. Near the top of each end wall, arrange a small door. Each fine, dry day, open one of these doors and the opposite trap, so that the air may circulate freely and keep the top dressing or covering of sawdust dry. This top dressing should not be too thick, from eight to twelve inches thick. The dressing must be looked after and kept dry at any cost. It will be found helpful, although troublesome, to divide the top layer of sawdust by a thick layer of newspaper.

PACKING AND KEEPING THE ICE

Packing the ice. The first layer of packing is commonly placed on edge rather than laid flat. There is no less waste that way, because, although each cake wastes less, there are more cakes on the floor. Sometimes this plan is followed throughout, with the advantage being that in breaking the ice, there is less adhering surface between the cakes. It is harder to pack this way, however; and the liability to undue side-wall pressure is greater. At least every third layer, no matter how packed, should be laid so as to break the joints of the previous layer that there may be no circulation through the mass.

The packing can be done up to within six inches of the side walls if a double wall is used, and up to within eight or ten inches with a single wooden side. As already stated, if concrete, stone, or brick, be used, there should be from ten to twelve inches left around the sides. In every case the space left should be filled with sawdust lightly tapped into place, but not rammed tightly. Hard tapping forces the sawdust down so solidly so as to remove most of the air, while light tapping keeps the mass porous but yet held together tightly enough to retain the air and prevent its escape or circulation.

Finally, it should be said that the cakes must be cut as true as possible with no small pieces or broken cakes allowed to enter the house. The ice should be packed in freezing weather so that the cakes will be dry and not freeze together in the house. Each cake should be kept an inch or an inch and a half from its neighbor on every side. Some ice dealers make a practice of filling this space with snow or broken ice so as to further prevent circulation of air through the ice. This has many advantages. It produces a huge solid cake of ice in the icehouse by reason of the weakness of the joints, but it makes "breaking out" of cakes comparatively easy.

Care of crop when stored. Whenever the icehouse is entered, warm air is necessarily admitted as the doors are open. The ventilators should then be open as the warm air will cause vapor to collect above the ice, and this should be permitted to escape at once. The dressing on the top will need occasional attention, as it must be kept dry. Drains should be inspected, to see that they are not clogged.

"Breaking out" the ice. As the ice is removed, the top dressing should be kept in place. It is usually a good plan to take cakes from a number of layers at one time, with the courses or layers being kept in a sort of a step-like series of tiers. The top tier should be worked back the farthest, the next layer not so far, and the third still less. This allows greater ease of operation in every way.

The cakes are usually pried out by a bent bar and separated from adjacent cakes of the same tier by a long-handled chisel, with both tools being specially made for such purposes. Occasionally, it is necessary to use a saw to separate the cakes at the sides. A special pointed saw is designed for this purpose.

COLD-STORAGE HOUSES FOR THE FARM

Advantage of cold storage. Most progressive farmers have learned the value of the individual icehouse on the farm, yet many have not realized that the most economical way of using the ice cannot be developed without a properly constructed cold-storage chamber. Creamery and cooperative cold-storage chambers are now quite common, and their importance is realized. As the farmer observes them in use for commercial purposes he will undoubtedly come to appreciate the value to him of a similar house at home built on a smaller scale.

The great advantage of cold-storage lies in the fact that produce does not need to be shipped to market immediately, but can wait a favorable time for a favorable market. This is especially true of fruit crops where the market is apt to be glutted during the usual delivery season. To wait for a few weeks will help to equalize the supply. What is true of market shipments is equally true of meat and produce for home consumption. Purchases may be made at a favorable time and in considerable quantity. The produce raised on the farm for home use can be held over a longer period and waste practically eliminated.

Insulation. The details of construction may, as in the case of the icehouse, be widely varied to suit particular needs. There are certain fundamental principles which can be laid down for guidance; however, close adherence is mandatory for successful construction. Satisfactory insulation can be obtained through the use of double walls for the cold–storage chamber. This provides a dead–air space between the walls, since that is the best form of protection. The air within the space must be dead air, and the walls must be airtight to give satisfaction. There are many other ways of insulating, like filling the space between walls with some so-called "non-conducting" substances, such as the following, (named in the order of their desirability): hair felt, slag wool, wood ashes, chopped straw, charcoal, cork, and others.

The insulating properties of these substances enclose small amounts of dead air which cannot escape in the tiny spaces between their individual particles. That air is the insulator. For this reason the substances cannot be packed solid, and they should be tapped lightly into place rather than rammed hard.

For cold-storage work, it should be borne in mind that there is more to be considered than merely keeping the products. They must be kept properly and untainted. Something must be chosen for insulation which does not readily absorb moisture and odors. There is no one substance which does not do this to some extent. If the building can be built with matched boards and the dead-air space lined with tarred paper, the space need not be filled with anything. In fact, a filling would be a decided detriment. Absolutely dead air is essential, however.

Detrimental effects of dampness. Moisture has the property of absorbing many gasses and impurities from the stores, so that it is very desirable that the air in the food chamber be kept as dry as possible and that the moisture which it does absorb be removed. In this way the air may be purified. The way in which this is accomplished is to provide proper circulation of the air in the storage chamber, thus cooling the stores by circulation of the cold air in contact with them rather than by radiation. Unless cooling is done in this way, the moisture which the air contains will be deposited on the stores and not on the ice. This, of course, will cause some of the packed material to become tainted.

Circulation of air. To secure a good circulation in the storage chamber, it is only necessary to understand that cold air falls and warm air rises. This means that the icebox must be above the level of the storage-space floors so that the cold air at the bottom of the storage space will provide an outlet and a return at the top of the chamber to allow the heated air to go back to be cooled and deprived of moisture.

For a small chamber, it will work best if the cold air is allowed to enter along the lower edge and the warm air taken out at the upper and diagonally opposite edge. This will make it necessary for the air to cross and circulate all through the storage space before reaching the outlet.

In a larger chamber, the cold air could be introduced

at the center of the floor and taken out at each of the upper side edges.

In a still larger room, the cold air may be introduced along two side edges at the bottom and allowed to pass through two side edges at the top.

Shields or deflectors, which may be made of wood painted with enamel, should be placed so as to prevent the cold air, as it warms up, from going from the inlet directly to the outlet without circulating through the room. These deflectors should slope from the bottom upward and be placed just over the cold-air inlets, so that as the cold air warms, it will rise along the deflectors toward the outlet. Care must be taken not to place the deflectors so as to pocket any warm air—that is, they should not be made so that any body of warm air will be caught in an upper corner and have to go downward to escape. Deflectors are necessary only where the outlet is nearly over the inlet and a path from one to the other does not lead through or near the center of the storage space.

Ventilation. Ventilation is essential; but, except in very large rooms, it is satisfactorily taken care of by the opening and closing of the entrance door.

Types of cold-storage houses. The usual cold-storage house is a two-story affair with the icebox on the second floor and storage chamber below. Flues are provided to admit the descending air at the bottom of the storage chamber, and to take out the warm ascending air from the top. The water from the melting ice is carried away in drains which must be carefully trapped and sealed as in the case of the icehouse.

The cold-storage house can be built like the icehouse, described above, as to foundations, walls, and roof. A solid foundation is essential with strong floor beams and posts. The walls and floor should be doubled with an air space to provide insulation. The top ceiling should also be doubled.

There should be a ventilator in the roof and a controlled opening through the ceiling of the icebox.

Temperature maintained. Usually the temperature best adapted for storage purposes is one set at four to ten degrees above freezing. The lower temperatures, 34-36 degrees, are generally used, but some fruits do better at a slightly higher temperature. For freezing meats and poultry, temperatures much below 32 degrees must, of course, be maintained. This is done by means of a salt refrigerating tank.

Refrigerating tank. In place of the ice-box, a water-tight sheet-metal tank is used. The tank must be fairly large in order to have a large radiating surface. There should be about four square feet of radiating surface to 25 cubic feet of cold-storage space. A drain is arranged for the tank, the bottom sloped toward the drain to allow the water to run off. As moisture condenses on the surface of the tank, provision must be made to drain the floor below. Usually a tray or pan is placed underneath. The tank is usually placed right in the cold-storage room, raised well above the floor. It is regularly supplied with ice and salt and, if properly cared for, will maintain a zero temperature.

Artificial refrigeration. There are numerous machines on the market for maintaining a low temperature without the use of ice. The method used is scientific. Ammonia, which is naturally a gas, is very highly compressed, its temperature lowered, and the ammonia liquefies. The liquid is allowed to escape through a tiny valve into expansion coils and, being relieved from pressure, it vaporizes again into a gas. This requires heat, just as when water is boiled. The heat is supplied to the ammonia from the surrounding objects and they become colder and colder as the process continues. This action is like that of any vaporizing liquid. If alcohol is dropped on the hand, the hand becomes cold as the alcohol vaporizes, because the alcohol abstracts the heat from the hand causing vaporization to take place.

In the case of ammonia, if the expansion coils are placed in brine, the heat will be abstracted from the brine, and the pans of pure water placed in the brine will be frozen. If the coil is placed in a cold-storage chamber, the temperature of the chamber will be lowered and kept lowered as long as the process continues. The ammonia gas is withdrawn from the expansion coils, compressed, and released again, and with a slight leakage, is used over and over again.

The process described is not always followed in every detail, but is typical of artificial methods.

Storage without ice. Root and fruit cellars are common in all parts of the country. A cave on the side of a hill is commonly used in New England for a potato cellar and, in southern Europe, similar caves in the mountain-sides have been used for the storage of oranges. The essentials of such cellars are dryness and proper ventilation. Dampness always promotes decay. A lack of ventilation will frequently result in sweating. The sweating of fruit and vegetables upon sudden removal from such a cellar or from cold storage, always takes place and the moisture formed must be removed before packing the produce for sale. To prevent sweating, the temperature of the produce must be gradually reduced to the temperature of the outside air.

For indoor storage of root crops, a sand covering is recommended. A dry floor is essential. A layer of sand is spread and then the roots are spread in layers, with each layer covered with sand. The storage space must be kept ventilated. In place of sand, sawdust or hay or excelsior and sometimes lime is employed. The whole object is to keep air away from the stored fruits or vegetables. Keep the air away, keep the produce dry, have good ventilation to prevent sweating, and a considerable degree of success is certain.

Packing stores. The packing of stores in cold storage is a science in itself and can be learned only by experience. One general rule, however, will take care of most difficulties, namely: pack the stores fairly close together and leave a space between them and the walls so as to allow a path for the circulating air. Never pack up close to the walls.

Duration of cold storage. It is difficult to give more than a general idea of the length of time for which any specific produce may be kept economically and profitably. This depends greatly on local conditions. Meats and fowl can be kept for 15 or 20 days and, when frozen, are, of course, frequently kept longer. Butter and eggs, cabbage, turnips, potatoes, etc., may be kept for months. Most fruits will keep a month; grapes, pears, watermelon, and citrus, will keep very much longer; and apples will even keep six months.

HISTORY OF ICE-MAKING
Unique Methods Followed by the Ancients.
Mount Joy Herald, October 15, 1898
from Lancaster Historical Society

The most ancient method of making ice is practiced in India. Holes are made in the ground, dry straw is put at the bottom of these, and on it, at the close of the day, are placed pans of water, which are left until the next morning when the ice that is found within the pans is collected. This industry is carried on only in districts where the ground is dry and will readily absorb the vapor given off from the water in the pans. The freezing, of course, is due to the great amount of heat absorbed by the vapor in passing from its liquid to its gaseous form.

Another process was practiced in the days of ancient Rome, when the wealthy are said to have had their wines cooled by having the bottles placed in water into which saltpetre was thrown, the bottles being the while rotated.

Dr. Cullen, in 1755, discovered that the evaporation of water could be facilitated by the removal of the pressure of the atmosphere, and that by doing this, water could be frozen. Nairn, in 1777, discovered that sulphuric acid would absorb the vapor of water if placed in a second vessel separate from that containing the water, but connected with it. This discovery he put to use in 1810 by constructing an apparatus for absorbing the vapor of the water that it was desired to cool or freeze. This apparatus greatly facilitated the freezing operations of a vacuum freezing machine.

Jacob Perkins was the father of what is now known as the compression system, having invented the first machine of the kind in 1834, and, as these machines, improved, are at the present day more in use than any other, a description of Perkins' patent may be of interest. His apparatus consisted of an insulated vessel, in which was enclosed a second vessel containing ether; a vapor pump, a worm and wormtub, a tube between the second vessel and the pump, another between the pump and the worm, a third between the worm and the bottom of the ether vessel, and the necessary valves.

As afterwards constructed, the apparatus was made up of a jacketed pan, within which was the water to be cooled; an insulated box, in which was placed the pan; a pump to extract the vapor from the jacket; a worm in which the vapor was condensed after it left the pump; a worm-tub containing cold water to cool the worm, and by means of the latter the vapor within it; and pipes connecting the top of the pan jacket to the pump, the pump with the upper end of the worm, and the lower end of the worm with the under side of the pan jacket. The refrigerating agent used with this apparatus was one derived form the destructive distillation of caoutchouc. James Harrison improved upon Jacob Perkins' apparatus in 1856, and it has been further improved by many others since.

PART II

Ice Harvesting

THE OLD ICE DAM

The ice pond was located a quarter of a mile north of Intercourse on Route 772—twenty feet from the bridge facing east. The dam was four to five feet in height, and ten to fifteen feet wide. It was half as large as the one at Mascot Mill, which is still standing today. The old dam was torn down in 1928 when they made another one approximately one hundred feet further up stream.

From the old dam, it had a three- to four-foot dirt ridge around the surrounding area in the meadow, about the size of one and one-fourth acre to hold the water and to make ice. It was also used to turn a water wheel that gave power to pump water out of the well that supplied the farm.

All running water pumped from the well, first went to the kettle house to keep the food cool. Then it went to the milk house to keep the milk cans cool until they were hauled away every morning, except on Sundays.

After the water cooled the milk, it went to the barn trough for the horses and cows. From there it went to the chicken house, and then from there, down to the meadow into the stream. Every farm that lived along a stream had a water wheel to pump water out of their well and to supply the farm. This dam and waterwheel was built in 1928. It was never used for ice harvesting.

ICE SKATING ACTIVITIES

Grandpa told me that on Sundays most of the Amish teenagers would ice skate on the ice pond, along the fence

...and Stories from the Older Folks

A waterwheel built in 1928 on our farm to pump water from the well. Never used for ice harvesting.

posts which lined the driveway where the horses were tied. When my Great-Grandfather would come home from visiting friends, he could barely get through the driveway. They would start a fire in the tobacco cellar to keep the kids warm. In the end, Great-Grandpa decided to put an end to the ice rinks by selling his ice equipment because the Amish kids and the kids from town would get a bit rebellious.

All of the ice equipment was sold to a man in Gordonville. Eighty years later, I saw this same ice equipment at a farm sale. Grandpa told me that it used to belong to my **Great-Grandfather**. I was so curious about the days of ice harvesting that I ended up buying the ice equipment.

ICE HARVESTING DAYS

There used to be a lot of ice ponds throughout Lancaster County, Pennsylvania, and the surrounding areas, including the northeastern states.

Where there wasn't a lake or a river, the men would bank water in the meadow about three to four feet in depth.

There were five icehouses in Intercourse, Pennsylvania. The ice was hauled to town from our meadow by horse- and mule-drawn sleighs and wagons.

WHERE WAS THE ICE-CUTTER MADE?

The ice-cutter has a wooden guard on the bottom to protect the bottom of the cutting tip. On the one corner is: Knickerbocker Ice Company, Sixth and Arch Street, Philadelphia.

Knickerbocker was a liquor at one time which also helped the market for ice harvesting. So in that case, if the ice melted in their drinks, they were drinking water from a river, lake, or stream.

On August 7, 1883, there was a fire at the stable and ice house of Knickerbocker Ice Company, Willow Street Wharf. Thirty-three horses and four mules burned to death, totaling a loss of $35,000. Reading freight depot had adjoining damage. This is the only history I could find on Knickerbocker Ice Company.

HAND TOOLS FOR ICE HARVESTING

Hand tools to harvest the ice included: Ice cutter (see photo), three saws, one ice hook, five tongs, one bar for "breaking out", and six ice cabinets or ice refrigerators. A block of ice would be put in the top left door. The cabinet has a small drain pipe in the bottom left to drain the melting water. It also has a small pipe through the kitchen wall for drainage. Every week you put another block in. Homemade ice cream in those days was almost the same as luxury, so I guess that classed where the name came from—ice and cream.

CUTTING THE ICE

First, you shoe the horse with cork shoes. Then, you went every eighteen inches with the cutter, length and cross

ways, like harrowing a garden. The first time over it, you only cut a half of an inch deep. Once you go over it two or three times, it requires less to cut with the handsaw.

One would cut a section of six to ten blocks, then stand on it and float with that section to the corner of the ice pond where they cut it finished at the ramp so they would not have to slide piece by piece across the pond to load on these sleighs. Getting these blocks off the ice after they were cut was a very dangerous project, especially on rivers and lakes.

When the sled was unloaded, it was returned to the ice bed to obtain another load, while some of the workers remained in the ice house to spread the sawdust. Frequently, if there were enough workers, there was more than one sled or wagon used to haul the ice. While one sled or wagon was unloaded at the ice house, the other was at another source being loaded. Ice harvesting was as important as getting in a corn crop.

Notice the three men pulling the rope in the photo on the next page! Ice houses along a pond, meant there would be long ramps. But at our farm, there was a short ramp that

came to the same height as the wagon bed. This picture is the same size as the five ice houses that were in Intercourse. One was located at Eby's Store (R.S. Worst). At the two taverns, Zimmerman's and Wanner's Bakery, which you could store eggs and food as well in the summer months. We also stored some ice in the west side of our barn in the corner of a little shed, which had tarred roofing paper around the walls. We packed in the sawdust which would also keep for a couple of months. Hardwood sawdust worked the best. Softwood, like pine etc., did not pack as snug.

BREAKING THE ICE

Summer, winter, spring, or fall—which do you like, best of all? As the cold winter months came again, they placed planks across the dam to back up the water in order to create a pond. As the temperature dropped around zero degrees, and the snow blowed on it, it was time to check and see how thick the ice was. When it reached between ten to twelve inches thick, it was time to get the crew. These were the days when the English and Amish folks helped each other harvest their

crops, cut trees, remove tree stumps, pick up rocks, butcher hogs, dig out cellars with dirt scoops, harvest ice, and so on.

The attitude was, "You go to your church, and I'll go to mine. And we all will look forward to a grand vacation in a better land than this." These gentlemen enjoyed nature.

As the big brawly men gathered with their frosty beards and mustache and heavy coats, there were the ice cutters heading for the ice pond with saws in their hands and temperatures in the single digits.

Wind from the north with the glittering ice off the sunshine, the first step was to see if there was any snow on the ice that had to be scraped off with a big scoop, similar to a dirt scoop that they used in those days.

When the snow was removed, then the plows started. The plow had two handles and almost looked like a garden cultivator. It also had a set of eight blades on the bottom. Each plow had a single horse or mule attached to it. As they started with the plow, it was cut every eighteen inches as a quarter of the pond. Then it was also cut crossway (checkered). Every eighteen inches was a cake. The plows went over it two or three times to make less cutting for the hand saws.

"All right men, here we go!" says a good natured gentleman. "You have a choice of keeping your saws going, or get frozen fast to the ice." With the smiling faces, these robust outdoor men, soon had a few sections cut. They would start a quarter of the way out, cut each cake separately, and then put the cakes on the ice. Then they slid the cakes to the ramp at the corner of the pond, where our driveway is now.

After the first quarter was finished, they would cut a section of six or eight cakes and stand on it with a pole. They would float with it until they reached the corner of the pond, and then cut each block separately. Grandpa was only nine years old then, but still remembers watching the men floating in with the ice to the loading ramp. They slid it up the ramp and into the sleighs.

SOME HAD ICE CELLARS

Ice was kept in improvised cellars, or in the portion of the cellar below the dwelling house when the family needed only small quantities of ice or if there was no icehouse. Some older folks said that ice was also stored beneath the barn floor. Sections of the floor would be removed and the ice buried in sawdust or in some other insulating material. Others told stories of how ice was stored beside the coldest stone wall in the barn structure. That is what they did on our farm.

When sawdust wasn't available, straw chaff or hay leaves were used as insulation, although these materials did not provide the protection that sawdust did. Occasionally water was poured over the ice after it was packed when the temperature was very cold. This consolidated the mass because the water froze solidly over it. However, this practice was not used too frequently because, with proper care, the ice kept well without resorting to this additional toil and sometimes loss. Proof of the effectiveness of the insulating material and method of storage was whether the ice could be kept until late fall from the previous winter.

ICE HARVESTING
Cutting Ice from the River January 13, 1912
from Lancaster Historical Society

The Susquehanna River begins in the hills above Cooperstown, New York, more than 400 miles away from McCall's Ferry in southern Lancaster County. Nowadays 400 miles of icebound river is unheard of. Utility plants will not allow the river to get that way. They pour warm water back into the river after using it to make electricity. Along the Susquehanna River at Rowenna there was a stone building 18x20 feet square with walls about 18 inches thick. It was so deep that it took a 10-foot ladder to get down to the last piece of ice or to climb from the bottom up to the first piece of ice. A great pile of sawdust was used to cover each layer of ice for insulation. Ice was needed for cooling milk and for making ice cream once a summer. It was always on a very cold day when the men would say, "I must go down to the river to see if the ice is thick enough to haul." If the ice was thick enough, they would take four to six men down. Often, because of their thick beards and mustaches, the men would come back inside covered with frost and looking pretty grizzly.

If it was snowing, they always brought the ice sheds, but if not, a two-horse wagon. The ice had to be sawed from the river. Sometimes they would make ice water from it.

ICE ICE

I have harvested 400 tons of pure clean natural ice, and as soon as this supply is exhausted I will have clean manufactured ice made from distilled spring water, guaranteed free of ammonia. Guaranteed to supply good ice the entire season.

WAGONS THROUGH MT. JOY AND FLORIN DAILY

See me before you place your order as prices are very reasonable.

C. S. Frank

Bell Phone   MT. JOY

1,200 TONS OF ICE

     I hereby wish to inform the public that I have housed 1,200 tons of pure spring water ice which I am prepared to serve at very moderate charges. Will run a wagon through Mount Joy and Florin daily. A share of your patronage is respectfully solicited as this is the finest crop housed in ten years. You can get ice at any time. I am also prepared to do all kinds of hauling and plowing at any time. Chas. Frank.

March 29, 1905

     — Squire McFadden has had seventeen teams employed all week, hauling ice from Nissley's dam, about four miles northwest of town. They manage to get to town about four o'clock in the morning with the first loads and on Friday the alley leading to the ice house was blocked for a square with the waiting wagons.

Mount Joy 1885

A NEW ICE MAN

Charles Frank has purchased 300 tons of spring water ice from Ezra Zercher of near towna will runa wagon through

Florin daily this Summer. Any person wanting ice will please call on or address Charles S. Frank, Mount Joy, Pa.

April 13, 1904
THE CONESTOGA AREA HISTORICAL SOCIETY
Letter from Ken Hoak/President/Curator

    The dam on the Conestoga River at Slackwater was built before the Civil War (approx. 1840s) as part of the Lancaster, Susquehanna, Slackwater Navigation Company's canal between Lancaster and Safe Harbor on the Conestoga River.

The dam provided a water reservoir for the operation of a lock to raise and lower canel boats. Later, the dam provided water power to operate the Schober Paper Mill. Still later, it provided to generate electricity from a small hydro-generating plant.

Ice, behind the dam, that formed in the reservoir lake was cut out and stored in a large ice house that was located beside the canal next to the Petersville Hotel, a stone structure (now a private home) still standing in Slackwater, approximately one mile south of Millersville. The house is in Conestoga Township, and the ice house stood beside the house, to the right.

REFRIGERATION IN LITITZ
1756-1956

"Pilgerhaus" built in 1862 by George Klein on the site of Hershey Apartments, Main Street, had one of the first of cooling systems (a spring house) located on its property.

Ice for the "ice box" era of Lititz came from the Bricker Ice Dams located north of Lititz. Warehoused in

Refrigeration in Lititz: Ice Wagon

sawdust during winter months, it was sold door to door from special built ice wagons as pictured above.

Through the years, different locations in the vicinity of Lititz were used as dam sites for the production of ice. Among many local people connected with the ice business were George Klein, John Schoenlein, John Bricker, John Yerger, Albert Gochenaur, Rueben Dull, Chester Ruth, and Ellis Kauffman.

The first artificial Ice Plant was built in Lititz in 1920 by Jacob Stober on the sight of a former Livery Stable in North Alley. He operated it until 1930 when it was purchased by J. M. Leed, the present owner.

With the advent of the electric refrigerator there is little demand for ice.

In 1938 the ice storage rooms were rebuilt and enlarged for zero storage to accommodate individual locker patrons and large bulk storage rooms.

Lancaster County vegetables are frozen and stored then shipped out in refrigerated trucks to cities on the eastern seaboard and as far west as Chicago.

Refrigeration from Spring to Zero Temperature.

J. M. Leed Locker Service
Lititz Bicentenial

HISTORICAL SKETCH OF REAMSTOWN, PENNSYLVANIA

(An exact reprint of our machine. In all it probability it was the same machine. This picture is in a book with Reamstown books.)
Immigrant and Mennonite Preacher, Johannes Stauffer

FROM MICHIGAN TO TEXAS

The railroads were also a good way for transporting ice. It took several tons to fill one car. Railroads changed a

This is an ice-sawing machine invented and manufactured by Abraham Lincoln Stauffer, the owner and operator of the Wabash Mill in East Cocalico Township. The early saw was operated by hand, as may be seen by looking at the picture. Later Mr. Stauffer improved his invention by installing a gasoline engine on the frame to run the saw. The above saw was invented about the year 1900.

lot of lifestyles when they figured out how to get ice all the way to Texas. I don't know how much it melted till it got there, but they started off with a three-hundred pound block.

They also had ice peddlers that had their regular routes. They could tell who wanted ice from the sign posted in the store's or home's window–it looked like a clock, except the hands pointed to how many pounds were needed instead of the time.

Wabash (Stauffers) Ice Dam, E. Cocalico Township.

McVey's Ice Dam, Ephrata, 1912. Historical Society of the Cocalico Valley.

Everybody had an ice cabinet. When you put the block of ice in the top left corner cold air flowed downward, keeping food in a second compartment below cool. As the ice melted it dripped down in a funnel, into a drain pipe.

After World War II, most of the people got electricity. One of the first things bought was a refrigerator. You could buy a refrigerator or an installment plan and pay less a month than they had paid for ice. There are still English folks living today that had no TV in their childhood days. As well as some older Amish folks that never made a phone call.

PART III

GREAT-GRANDFATHER

AUCTION ACCOUNT

This is an account of the personal property from a farm sale, which was a great-grandfather of my grandpa. This sale was held in the spring year of 1880.

Notice: Only had $41.40 cash evening of the sale.

Levi King	Jockey stick	.04
L. E. Fisher	Stamper	.13
L. E. Fisher	2 Single Trees	1.00
Jacob Fisher	Horn Anvil	.18
L. E. Fisher	Jack screw	.75
L. E. Fisher	Digging Iron	.65
L. E. Fisher	Crow bar	1.30
John Draner	Bag wagon	.35
Daniel Esh	Half bus	.10
Geo Bear	Manure fork	.35
Michael Smoker	Wash Machine	.03
David Pleam	Seat	.11
Daniel Esh	Seive	.20
Abram Stoltzfus	Double tree	.45
Christian Esh	Shake fork	.05
L. E. Fisher	Manure drag	1.00
L. E. Fisher	Hay fork	1.00
Jacob E Fisher	Barn shovel	.44
J. K. Beiler	Double tree	.02
John Drener	2 forks	.02
L. E. Fisher	Shake fork	.03

L. E. Fisher	2 Scrapers	.01
D. Pleam	2 Rods	.12
D. Pleam	Lot	.02
L. E. Fisher	Lot	.04
C. B. Lapp	2 Hay forks	.62
Jacob Esh	Grain fork	.31
Daniel Esh	Grain fork	.05
L. E. Fisher	Grain fork	.05
A. N. Diller	Grain fork	.15
Daniel Esh	Grain fork	.10
David Pleam	Grain fork	.03
L. E. Fisher	Dung Hook	.13
Philip Troup	Barn shovel	.31
L. E. Fisher	2 Hand rakes	.50
Daniel Esh	3 Rakes	.18
Jonas Zook	Hay knife	.10
L. E. Fisher	Hay rake	.70
D. Pleam	Hay hoister	.31
D. Esh	2 Grain bags	.36
L. E. Fisher	2 Grain bags	.30
L. E. Fisher	2 Grain bags	.50
L. E. Fisher	2 Grain bags	.40
Jacob Fisher	2 Grain bags	.62
L. E. Fisher	2 Grain bags	.60
Jacob E. Fisher	2 Grain bags	.40
Daniel Esh	2 Grain bags	.62
Daniel Esh	2 Grain bags	.20
Daniel Esh	2 two bus bags	.20
Jacob E. Fisher	2 two bus bags	.62
Jonas Zook	double tree	1.00
L. E. Fisher	double tree	3.50
Benj Beiler	double tree	.75
L. E. Fisher	log chain	1.75
L. E. Fisher	1 flynet	3.25
L. E. Fisher	sprader	.75

...and Stories from the Older Folks

* * * * *

John Diener	Brass Kettle	.87
Isaac Lapp	Cider Mill	4.50
Daniel Esh	Hay Ladders	1.75
L. E. Fisher	Corn Maker	5.00
Jacob Esh	Spike Harrow flat	1.50
L. E. Fisher	Spike Harrow flat	1.00
Isaac Muckle	Spike Harrow flat	.75
Geo Skiles	Shovre Harrow	.25
Philip Troup	Shovre Harrow	.25
L. E. Fisher	Shovre Harrow	3.25
L. E. Fisher	Cultivator	1.00
D. Pleam	Landis Plow	.60
John Z. Lapp	Plank plow	.70
Jonas Zook	Wiley plow	1.50
L. E. Fisher	Cyra ? plow	8.00
L. E. Fisher	Wallace plow	9.00
Amos Leaman	Root plow	3.25
L. E. Fisher	Field Roller	11.00
L. E. Fisher	Grain Drill	17.00
L. E. Fisher	Cart	23.00
David Smoker	Shafts	.25
C. B. Lapp	Sled	5.50
David Smoker	Sled Bell	3.75
John L. King	Buggy body	2.00
D. Pleam	Sleigh box	.01
L. E. Fisher	Sled	2.75
L. E. Fisher	W? rake	20.00
Gideon B. Stoltzfus	Doulbe Shovel Harrow	1.50
L. E. Fisher	Pat Double Shovel Harrow	24.75
Philip Troup	Buggy	15.00
Jacob Esh	Spring Wagon	7.50
Jacob Esh	Wagon Pole	1.75
C. B. Lapp	Farm Wagon	10.00
L. E. Fisher	Hay Ladders	4.50

Jonas Zook	Horse Power	57.50
Jonas Zook	Jack	17.00
L. E. Fisher	Reaper	15.00
Jacob Esh	Separator	44.00
L. E. Fisher	65 ft. belt	20.15
Christ Esh	76 ft. belt	4.56
L. E. Fisher	Grain fan	9.50
Ephraim Siegle	3 sieves	.38
L. E. Fisher	Road wagon	25.00
L. E. Fisher	Wagon bed	14.00
L. E. Fisher	2 Shoats	8.00
L. R. Rhoads	2 Shoats	5.60
L. E. Fisher	Sow	13.00
Philip Troup	Sow	12.00
L. E. Fisher	Red cow and calf	40.00
Jonas H. Weaver	old cow and calf	23.50
J. K. Lapp	Dark red cow	35.00
Amos Hershey	Roan cow	25.00
A. E. Sellers	Roan Heifer	26.13
L. E. Fisher	Calf	12.00
Amos Leaman	2 Steers	83.00
Isaac Kreider	2 Steers	88.25
Geo Bair	3 chairs	1.17
		41.50
Daniel Esh	Bull	31.00
Daniel Esh	chair	.31
C. B. Lapp	Brown Horse	187.00
Eli Stoltzfus	Black Mare	150.50
Elias E. Fisher	Halter	.80
Elias E. Fisher	Black Colt	143.00
Howard Pierce	Black Mare	146.00
L. E. Fisher	Dog	2.10
	TOTAL	**1,625.24**

BILLS UNPAID

David Pleam	3.04
Philip Troup	31.06
Daniel Esh	36.71
Elias Stoltzfus	150.50
Christian Esh	4.51
Elias E. Fisher	145.10
Jonathan King	.25
Jacob E. Fisher	1.46
C. B. Lapp	240.50
Jacob Esh	56.56
Isaac Lapp	4.50
Christian Glick	.59
Isaac Muckle	.75
L. R. Rhoads	5.60
Gideon B. Stoltzfus	1.50
A. E. Sellers	26.13
Howard Pierce	146.00
L. E. Fisher	328.95

NOTES

Jonas H. Weaver	23.50
Amos H. Hershey	25.00
Amos Leaman	83.00
Benj Kreider	22.86
Isaac Kreider	129.75
Jonas Zook	81.09
John K. Lapp	35.00

Cash	41.41
Bills unpaid	1183.71
Notes	400.20

TOTAL   **1625.32**

A FARMERS DIARY
1880 until early 1900's

JANUARY

January 5 - Started school. Shelled corn. Butchered hog, weighed 815 lbs., and beef. Took hide to New Holland. Fetched a load of apple wood with the sled.

Went to Lancaster to buy steers.
Cleaned chicken roost.
Fetched the doctor for one of the girls.
Chopped corn for bedding.
Washed the cattle with tobacco juice.
Took tobacco to Lancaster with sled.
Went to Farmersville Store with the lard, got 8¢ lb. Fetched a bad off colt.
Opened the lane behind the house.
Shot sparrows. Shelled seed corn. Made a stall in the steer stable.
Went to Intercourse horse sale.
Went to Bird-In-Hand to sell wheat – 83 cents a bushel
Afternoon took mules to shop. Stripped tobacco.
In Lancaster with butter – to 27¢ lb.
10° below zero.
Killed 3 hogs. 4° above zero. Took wheat to Gordonville.
On Mine Ridge for a load of post.
Hauled lumber from Bareville; 14 teams were hauling.
Unloaded 2 car loads in the woods. Burned brush. Worked in woods. Sawed down trees, then dragged log to mill.
Killed 5 hogs.

FEBRUARY

Baled tobacco. It rained.
Went to Bareville for clover seed; paid 4.75 a bushel.

Fetched a load of post at Mime Ridge; 40 posts with the sled, in the afternoon a load of 33 posts.
Chopped corn.
Hauled tobacco to Lancaster; 2 tons, got 16¢ lb., 4¢ lb., 2¢ a lb.
Went to Farmersville with hog meat; 8¢ lb. for lard; 10¢ lb. for sausage; 4¢ lb. for tallow.
Fetched coal at Bird-In-Hand; 900 lbs.
Took butter to Bareville.
Hung meat up.
Took tobacco to Lancaster.
Dehorned a cow.
Fetched bran at Bareville.
Killed a steer.
Hewed post.
Cold, worked in the woods. Blew out stumps. Greased harness. Cut down walnut tree. Blew out the walnut stump with dynamite.

MARCH

Thrashed 162 bu. wheat.
It snowed all day.
Baled tobacco all afternoon.
Split wood all day.
Took tobacco to Honey Brook; got 12¢ lb., 8¢ lb., 4¢ lb., 2¢ lb.
Big snowstorm. Afteroon opened the road.
Fetched coal at Ephrata. Cut trees at the line.
Made an axe handle. Burned brush. School stopped.
We were quarrying stones.
In Lancaster with apples; got 15 half peck at 1.00 a bu. Got 27¢ lb. For butter.
Hewed post.
Shelled corn. Shelled seed corn.

Aftrnoon hewed post.
Unload 2 cars of lime in Bareville. Dragged road 3 1/2 hours.
Seed clover seed.
Dragged road 1 1/2 hour. Burned brush and stumps at the woods.
Dehorned 3 steers. Worked in the shop. Made a maul.
Dragged road 2 hours.
Made a hand dug well.

APRIL

Picked up stones.
Baled tobacco.
Took tobacco to Lancaster.
Hauled manure.
Took black cow to New Holland.
Fetched a bushel clover seed in New Holland. Sowed clover seed.
Made fence at the school house.
Marked out for potatoes.
Burned brush until dinner.
Shelled seed corn.
At the Blacksmith shop with the mules.
Greased harness
At Mine Ridge for a log to build chicken shed.
Planted potatoes.
Put down a tree behind house.
Afternoon, dragged the public road.
Took two mare colts to Spring Garden, two to Intercourse, seven to Stasburg.
Dragged road.
Took butter to Bareville. Took bull away, $44.78.
At Bards for dynamite. Got 50 lbs. at 26¢ a lb.
Blew stumps to fix road.
Canel was here to blow stumps until 2:00, then I burnt

stumps and shut the holes.
Afternoon burned stumps.
In New Holland for dynamite. Blew stumps until 2:00, then piled up rails.

MAY

Took butter to Bareville.
Fetched a calf, 140 lb. At 4 1/2¢ a lb., $6.30.
Marked out for corn. Afternoon planted corn.
Made fence in the lane. Fetched a load of wood at Welsh Mountain.
Took wheat to Bird-In-Hand; 92¢ for 72 bu.
Fetched a load of lumber home.
Hauled sand.
Fetched a load of shingles.
Sold wheat at 92¢ a bushel. 70 bu. 33 lbs.
Got the chicken manure ready for the tobacco patch.
Made sweet potato rows.
Fetched a load of lumber at Bird-In-Hand.
Fetched a load of bricks at Voganville.
Fetched bran.
Carpenters here; worked at barn.
Sold steers.
Sold 12 bu. seed corn at 65¢ a bu.
Spread lime. Fanny got a colt.
At the fishenshore all day.
Started home from the fishenshore; came home about midnight.
Peddled shad until dinner.
Fetched a barrel of sugar.
Sow got pigs.
Took a fat hog to Lancaster.
Dragged road.
Made a latch for the little door.

JUNE

Took butter to Bareville.
Afternoon dragged the public road.
Shoveled corn.
Bought 2 sows.
Fetched a load of rails at Mine Ridge. Fetched a load of post on Mine Hill.
Made a fence a long the lane. Raised neighbor shed.
Fetched a load of stone.
Put new shovel on cultivator. Picked cherries.
Sharpened the reaper knife. Cut grass. Made hay.
Put a handle in the big fork. Cut wheat all day.
Worked on the road.
Fixed corn crib. Cut wheat. Tied wheat.
Hauled in wheat all day; 13 loads.
Worked for the Township; hauled stone.
Got fly nets. Got barrel sugar; 362 lb. At 5¾¢.
Took butter to Bareville.
Took out stumps. Dragged road 1½ hour. Dragged logs to sawmill.
Dehorned 6 cattle.
Went to Bird-In-Hand. Fetched 1 barrel oil from station.
Trimmed trees in the orchard.
Hauled dirt from the road on barn bridge.
Made ice cream in the evening.
Doll got a colt.

JULY

1838 – the reaper was invented.
Made cigars. 1848 - first cigars wrapper farmed in Lancaster County.
Thrashed rakins. Fetched a load of coal. Hauled out manure. Plowed sod.

Plowed until 9:00. Plowed. Plowed. Making fence. Hauled in oats.
Suckered corn. Tied wheat until 9:00; 15 loads.
Hewed post all day. Evening took butter to Bareville.
Fetched the spring wagon in New Holland.
Started making hay. Sold old hay; got 28 loads.
Two cows hit by lightning.
Fetched ice to make ice cream from New Holland.
Spread dung in the afternoon.
Worked at the wheat took shocks apart.
Scooped dirt out of the lane field up around barn.
Hauled out dung; 14 loads. Raked Rankins.
Dug a bed for celery at the lower end of the garden.
Suckered corn.

AUGUST

Went to Intercourse with butter; 20¢ a lb.
Fetched coal in Bareville to thresh wheat.
In Lancaster got paint and oil to paint barn.
Took out potatoes.
Spread manure all day.
Fetched 2,100 cigars. Took the reaper apart cleaned the tobacco shed out.
White washed barn.
Finished plowing sod. Took out potatoes. Got the separator ready to thrash.
At Gordonville for tobacco scaffold.
Burned brush.
Thrashed all day.
Thrashed all day.
Oats and wheat.
Took wheat at Bird-In-Hand; 91 bu. at 92¢.
1888 got a part for the sulky plow.
Fetched the buggy at Abe Groff's.

ABC Groff in New Holland.
Dragged the public roads 3 hours.
Boys suckering tobacco.
Boy came home from Atlantic city.
We were hauling hay in Lancaster City.
Bought two cows to replace the two that were hit with lighting.
Went to Lancaster with trolley.
Suckered tobacco afternoon cut 8 ½ loads.
Picked apples plowed wheat stubbles.
Took a load of rubbish to mine hill lane.
Blowed out stumps.
Evening had Ice cream.
Mowed weeds all day.

SEPTEMBER

Was in Reading.
Got the seed wheat ready.
Cleaned it in the mill with corn for mush.
Plowed tobacco roots out.
Thrashed out 300 bushels wheat.
Cut off corn.
Took Kate in the shop.
Afternoon at sale in Intercourse for ponies
Took Lucy in the shop.
Afternoon at sale in Mechanicsburg had colt sale.
Fetched a lot of chickens.
At Franklin County for five bushels seed wheat.
Sowed wheat, picked apples, thrashed rye.
Sowed wheat, plowed in the tobacco patch with a horse.
Took Bill in the shop, got ready to go for sweet potatoes.
Went to Williamton, Delaware for Sweetpotatoes.
Oct. 4, 1887
Started home with our potatoes.

Came home in evening at half past nine o'clock.
Two day trip, Oct. 5, 1887 from Lancaster Co. to Delaware.
Canned the potatoes.
Made four barrels, Oct. 6, 1887.
I made two barrels of cider today.
Boiled apple butter, got apple butter ready for market.
Took cider and apples to Lancaster.
Nine cents per gallon for cider.
$1.00 a bushel for apples.
Boys were cutting corn.
Took black sow to neighbor.
Boiled apple butter.
Made cider, 40 gallons.

OCTOBER

Carried potatoes in the cellar.
Harrowed all day.
Fetched a load of wood.
Fetched a load of coal.
A Bird-in-Hand to trash.
Afternoon got the separator.
Read to thrash.
Sowed the meadow, the other side.
Made apple butter, 10 crocks.
Made cider, thrashed all day, 220 bushels of oats, 103
    bushels of oats.
Thrashed all day, 265 bushels of wheat, sowed wheat,
    shelled corn.
Sold colt for $110.
Took wheat at Bird-In-Hand.
103 bushels, 76 cents. Per bushel.
Fetched a load off cole home
3,8500 pound hard nut at $4.50 a ton.
Killed a hog.

Husked corn
Hauled manure out of hog pen
Killed a hog
Bought sucking pigs for .5 a piece
Made cider
Boiled apple butter
Husked corn
Fetched a barrel of oil and sugar
Made two barrels of cider
Sold two barrels of cider
Afternoon at Intercourse
Calf sale
Sold black hog

NOVEMBER

On market in Lancaster with apples and cider
.12 for apples
.12 cents for gallon cider
husking corn on the hill for gate post
hauled in fodder three loads
made fence
around the barnyard
put a gate post in at the lane
got wagon shed ready for corn
killed a hog
took old gate post out
hauled fodder seven loads
bought a bull
afternoon fetched the bull a Monterey
fetched a load of railes
took 60 bushels wheat
at Bird-in-Hand
got 105 a bushel
hauled apple wood in the shed

greased the harness
in Lancaster for cole oil
Thrashed 240 bushel wheat
Fixed the road
Made a mall to split wood and a pigeon coop
Cut down apple trees
Sawed wood all day
Fetched the corn sheller
Shelled corn afternoon in Lancaster for apples
Fetched two barrels
Killed a steer
Hauled wood out of orchard
Cut down an apple tree
Along the road and cut it up
Bought five steers
Shelled corn
Took the dung out of the hog pen
At wedding
Rained all day shot sparrows
Thanksgiving Day was a meeting (church) made 3 barrels of cider
Took 3 barrels of cider to Lancaster city
Made 3.5 barrels of cider
Husked corn 56 shocks.

DECEMBER

Took butter to Bareville
Made a meat bench
Planted chestnut trees
Afternoon at Blue Ball to get the horse power tread fixed
Cought 43 pigeons
Killed 3 hogs
Afternoon at Landisvalley
Piled wood on the wood pile

Took girls to school
Took load of wheat to Bird-in-Hand
Got 102 cts a bushel
Fetched cole along home for the tobacco shed
2190 lb
cut wood on the mine hill
in Lancaster with ducks, pigeons, chickens
7 cents for ducks
7 cents for chickens
25 cents a piece for pigeons
Afternoon in Farmerville with land rat 10 cents
Bought Frank the bay house for $210
Took Bill in the shop
Afternoon took 151 pound lard in the store got 7.5 cents a pound
Fetched 900 lb off cole a Ephrata.
Too kout two loads of manure
Worked on the wood pile
Took out 8 loads manure
Sold calves
Got 6.5 a 5 ct a lb
Afternoon a Petersburg to order a wagon
Snowed 18 inches
Got the big sled out
Opened the road
Took scholars to school
Killed two hogs
Hauled tobacco stolks out
Shelled corn
Took girls to school
It rained in the mill with wheat for flour
Hung up the meat
Sold four pigs $4.00

Diary of Great-Grandfather

Great-Grandfather's barn burned to the ground on February 1, 1909. Here is his diary about the rebuilding process:

March 4, 1909 – Went to Mifflin Co. to look for slate at Uncle Joe Kurtz's. Colts were at Aaron Snyder's and then to Ben King's a couple of steers at George Buler's—a colt at Henry Dilinger's.

May 5, 1909 – Uncle Joe Kurtz came to help at the barn. They finished unloading 11 loads of slate in the front car.

May 9, 1909 – Fetched Gutters from Wrightville.

Hearsay – Fetched 40-feet long wooden beams from Wrightville along Susquehanna River. They were floated down from further up stream. They were hauled with four horses with a wagon gear. (They took the center pole out of the gear, then tied the wheels fast to the wooden beams.) Then were hauled through Lancaster City to Intercourse, Lancaster County.

May 12, 1909 – Unloaded the rest of the lumber. Punched holes in the slate for a few days.

May 1-15, 1909 – Concreted.

May 17, 1909 – Carpenters started to frame the barn.

May 28, 1909 – 30 people showed up to put up the girders and joists.

June 8, 1909 – Put the weather boarding on the barn.

June 10, 1909 – Put slates on the roof.

July 30, 1909 – Dug the foundation for the silo. Finished.

August 2-5, 1909 – Put up scaffold to start building silo. Almost done with silo. Finished the silo except for the roof. Started to pain silo.

August 18, 1909 – Started to dig foundation for engine house.

August 24, 1909 – Work on engine house.

August 28, 1909 – Slating the engine house.

Part IV

THE BEACON LIGHT

The Beacon Light was used to guide airplanes at nighttime. It was built in 1931. It was an impressive structure, twelve square feet, and about seventy feet tall. An iron ladder led to the top. At each corner of the Beacon Light there were four-foot plates anchored to a concrete base. At the center was a control box for the light setting. We would put our heads against the box to hear it ticking. Every month a service man would re-set the timer during the daytime.

When the service men climbed the tower they could feel it shake. When they reached the top there was a four-foot square platform with a pipe railing. The bright Beacon Light was five feet high, for most men, right at eye level. The brilliant light could be seen for miles. The light was so bright that it guided Grandpa on his journey home. The flash was so bright it flooded Grandpa's bedroom. He never needed to use a lantern when he was dressing for his day!

Grandpa and the other children were not allowed to leave the dinner table until they finished eating. But as soon as they heard an airplane they all went outside to watch it pass overhead. It's amazing how much air travel has changed over the years. Now there are military planes that can travel faster than the speed of sound. This all happened in one person's lifetime.

The Beacon Light eventually went dark. About 1958 it was torn down.

A view of the Beacon Light (top left), from Route 340. Picture from the Intercourse 200th Anniversary Book.

BEACON LIGHTS

I only know of three Beacon Lights:
    1. Mount Joy
    2. Beacon Hill, north of Intercourse
    3. Coatsville, south of Rt. 30

BEFORE THERE WERE ANY BUILDINGS ON BEACON HILL

    Levi Smoker lived along Route 772 where Centerville Road starts. The tract of his property was on the west side of Beacon Hill Drive. This was when the lane (road) was only used for the Beacon Light and for a farm lane for our farm. Levi had a harness shop, and raised tobacco plants to sell. He had 10 to 15 beds up behind his building. He also farmed about two acres of tobacco. In the spring when Grandpa was a boy, he would help Levi steam the beds with a Sig Steamer engine. When the whistle would blow, he would help change pans.

In the Fall when the tobacco was ready to harvest he also wanted some help. He hung all his tobacco in Intercourse. Back then, every home owner had a horse barn. The tobacco was hung it wherever there was room. Some rails were round and not nailed fasten. In those small barns, they were soon filled.

Grandpa still remembers when some English folks drove horses in town for transportation. Not exactly sure what this Gentleman's name was, heading for Lancaster, he would go down the road in his open buggy playing his guitar and singing away in the dust.

After Levi Smoker, Jacob Ebersole bought the land. He had a chair shop but the rest of the hill had no buildings. Jacob also had sheep once even numbering 100 sheep when they had lambs in one spring. It was a nice scene. They would come down the hillside and, as soon as they heard a little noise, they put their heads up and over the hill they went. What a sight.

Then the hill was sold in different lots. Harvey Good had some greenhouses then. Soon he made it into a campground. Harvey later sold it to Howard Lehr, then Bob and Joan Miller, and now Cliff and Renie, all were good neighbors.

Part V

BAKE OVEN

The inside was lined with brick, stone, and mortar. The height was approximately six feet high and five feet wide at the bottom. Tapered at the top, from the bottom, three feet high was a floor or similar to a shelf. It had two doors; 1) for the ashes; and 2) a door for the bake goods. Inside the baker's door was a one-foot square hole on the floor. The first step was to fill it up with wood, tree branches, old cracked wooden barrels—any kind of wood until it was full.

Then, burn it to ashes, scrape the ashes down the hole with a scraper, hoe type, as seen on the picture, as it was very hot. Then you'd get the pie shovel with a five-foot handle and fill the floor right up with pies.

A lot of chicken roasts were made for weddings and pies for church. They did not make much bread because it took too much wood. The home-made bread was made in the kitchen range. In the late 1930s and early 1940s people got gas kitchen stoves. The first ones were kerosene.

These were the days before carpet, paneling, and drywall. They put a few bricks in the kitchen range overnight. Then the next morning they stood on them to wash their breakfast dishes to keep their feet warm. They had no running water in the house, except a hand pump. In the coldest nights if you left a glass of water in the sink it was frozen until morning.

Outside bake oven attached to summer house.

1. Foot corn cutter.
2. Milk cans and strainer.
3. Cow chain.
4. Cow kicker chain.
5. Pie Shovel with a five foot handle.
6. Ashes scrapper (hoe type) with a five foot handle.
7. Hay knife.
8. Butter churn.
9. Milk stool.

Part VI

GRANDMA AND GRANDPA

IN THE 18TH CENTURY

On Sundays, they had meeting (church). The next day, they put the benches up in the attic since they did not have a bench wagon to store the benches. Benches would be shared when there was a funeral or wedding.

Neither were there enough books for everyone. Usually, the older ones didn't use books.

Sometimes they could not take all their children along in the winter, because there weren't enough Sunday shoes. They walked a lot, and also rode horse back.

One Sunday morning, a couple couldn't figure out why their son would not come in from the barn after morning chores. As the mother went to see where her son was, she found him fixing the saddle on his horse. His mother replied, "Son, you are not going to church with that saddle; but you can go bare-back. Me and my husband are going to walk." I guess that's the reason there is a slit on the over coats in the back, for it was designed for horseback riding.

BY TROLLEY, HORSE, AND WAGON

While we went to Lancaster in those years, there were very few cars. Bread and milk were delivered by horse and wagon or by men walking on the streets.

Trolley tracks went up the main street for transportation. People were too poor to have cars and some didn't think it was right to have cars. Country roads had ditches a foot or more deep in the February thaw. We used to walk in those ruts. When the roads dried up, the township had a drag to level the roads. When I was going to school they spread cinder on the road, which we appreciated in the early 1920s.

When Grandpa was a boy they would take the train from New Holland to Supplee near Honeybrook to visit his Uncle Seth. Uncle Seth eventually bought a farm on Colonial Road, one-fourth mile east of Intercourse. So when Uncle Seth moved in the spring of 1928, Grandpa was only fourteen years old. He and his cousins would drive fourteen cows twelve miles from Supplee to Cambridge on Route 340 (the Old Philadelphia Pike) until they came to Colonial Road.

Before the long trip, the cows were left in the barn and then led out into the twenty-acre meadow. The cows would put up a fight, kicking and jumping, but eventually they cooperated. Before they headed out, Uncle Seth would throw fifty cents on the ground and would tell them to buy themselves a snack along the way. They would stop in Cambridge to buy a big candy bar, which, at that time, was only 5 cents a piece! Then, they would head to White Horse. They would have the cows settled into their new home before dark. At that time, Al (Owl) Eby lived along Colonial Road. He would hitch a bull to a spring wagon to fetch feed for his cows.

It was located at Queen Road and Route 772. Earl Ames had the feed mill and Scott Pawell had a milk creamery, both in the same building. Grandpa would take his father's milk to the creamery every morning.

Al was a bachelor. His Amish neighbors helped him thresh wheat. His two old maid sisters lived with him. They were good cooks who would have the noontime meal on the table without fail. The house was a bit dirty though. When everyone went into the house for lunch there used to be a rooster perched on the kitchen range. On Sunday morning, he had his team of horses in the field. Grandpa wasn't sure how much wheat Al farmed but Uncle Seth had sixty acres. They would fill the barn and then thrash it out. This would continue until the wheat harvest was over.

WORKING ON DAD'S FARM

Before Grandpa began farming on his own, he would take his father's potatoes to Lancaster city to sell. He would tie up his horse one block from the town square. It cost twenty-five cents to board a horse for a day. After he took care of the horse, he would peddle his potatoes. The good customers would buy two to three bushels. Then Grandpa would help them carry them down to their cellars. Those were the days when everyone had big market wagons. On Sundays, people went to church in open carriages.

GRANDPA'S NEW HORSE

When Grandpa started farming, he went to Leola to get a ride on the trolley cars. He would head off to Ephrata. A man by the name of Bill Levers had a sale at that time. This was before the New Holland sales stables began. Grandpa saw a horse he liked, but he thought the price was too high, so he decided not to buy it. Frank Mower was a dealer who ended up buying the horse. Later that spring, Frank had a sale of all the cows, horses, and equipment that he had bought at previous farm sales. He lived below Strasburg. So Grandpa went to the sale in Strasburg. As soon as he arrived, he spied the horse he had admired at Bill Lever's place. He bought the horse for $25.00 less than Bill Lever's asking price. He hadn't had to feed it that winter, either. Grandpa rode his newly-purchased horse home that day.

AUNT MATTIE'S STRAW HATS

Aunt Mattie made straw hats, and I remember going along to help with the straw the day of the straw frolic. To get it to meet each knot of the rye stalks, the knots were cut off on each side of the knot. Mother used to bring some home to lie out on the lawn to bleach for hats. When a storm or rain came, we gathered it quickly, which was quite a task until the cut stalks were bleached.

When it got windy, the straw blew around, so tobacco lath were laid on top to keep the straw from getting mixed up. When it was dry enough, we stripped the straw to make it smooth and ready to plad for hats.

DOOR-TO-DOOR WITH THE
FRUITS OF OUR LABOR

Dad grew potatoes and in the fall he took them to Lancaster city in the market wagon. I remember getting up at 4:00 a.m. to go with him. We would go from door to door on the main streets, ringing door bells, and asking if anyone needed apple butter, cider, butter, or potatoes.

At that time no one had fire in their cellar or basement, so they took one- or two-hundred pounds of potatoes so they would have them for the winter. Dad took orders and went each Friday until he filled all his orders. Sometimes he also took apples along. It was quite a relief when all the potatoes were dug by a potato plow, because no potato diggers were available.

TO ZIMMERMAN'S WE GO

Our Great-Aunt Lizzie King owned the farm where Dad moved in the spring of 1912. They only had a couple milking cows, either Brindle's or Gurnsey's, that made more cream for butter to sell, which Dad took to Zimmerman's Store in Intercourse, Pa. They used to separate the milk. The separator had two spouts 5-6 inches long, one for cream, the other for skimmed milk which we emptied into different containers. No separators were used on Sunday mornings.

MORE OF GRANDPA'S STORIES

Boby candy for the small children came in 2-ounce bags (ten cents worth). These were the days of the depression. I remember when eggs were so expensive that we couldn't afford to eat them every morning. When we did have eggs for breakfast, we could only have one each.

We had fried mush and puddings made from pigs that Dad had raised. We also had bacon, and our cereal was oatmeal. In later years, after the Depression, Dad bought shredded wheat for a hearty breakfast before going to church. We only had shredded wheat with browned butter and hot milk on Sunday mornings. We were also given soft-boiled eggs to go along with the shredded wheat.

Mother seldom went to the store. When she needed organdy for aprons and caps to go to church, she sent a sample with Dad. When she needed everyday fabric, Dad would buy a bolt of black and white Lancaster gingham. All of our everyday dresses were made of gingham. The same fabric was used for the aprons we wore everyday. At that time, small children and adults wore aprons every day. In the summertime during the Depression, the women wore gingham dresses to church.

In wintertime we had wool batiste which couldn't be washed. Then in the 1930s, other fabrics became available.

GRANDMOTHER'S STORIES

During the winter we ate a lot of apples. Dad was one many farmers who had apple orchards at that time. Back then, spraying was not needed. Every season, there were a new variety of apples. When we were hungry, my mother would peel and slice apples and put them on a plate for us to eat. She also made apple cider and canned the apples as well. Mom would also make apple butter. In addition to the apples, Dad would also prepare for the long winter by filling the cellar with potatoes.

We had no pretzels at that time other than on Saturday. Dad got one-half pound for the little ones for church.

Each farmer had laying hens. I think we had between 100-200. Dad took our eggs to the store to pay store bills.

Mother hardly ever left home except when she went to her parents, Ben and Nancy, who lived across the field from us, where Maurice Good lived. We lived on a farm owned by mother's Great-Aunt Lizzie, Grandad's sister.

Dad went to visit his parents quite often in the evenings. One time while we were at Grandpa's, I fell asleep, so they left me there for the night. That was quite a treat for me because Grandma had eggcups. She would soft boil the eggs and cut the tops off. We dipped strips of bread into the egg yolk. We never did that at home! The next time we went to Grandpa's, I tried to act like a possum laying on the couch pretending that I was asleep. I was disappointed when my plan didn't work and I missed my Grandmother's eggs.

There were never many toys at our grandparent's house. They had building blocks, puzzles, and tiddly winks. Very few children had scrapbooks. I really can't remember any of the games except the tiddly winks. We always knew that when we were at our grandparent's house we couldn't run in the house.

Grandpa King had a small coal bucket six inches around and five inches deep. It was so nice to play with. We often went out into the yard where there was a path of crushed stones instead of concrete walks. We loved to put them in the coal bucket. Sometimes we dropped some of the stones in the grass which Grandmother didn't like. She came to the door and spoiled our fun. When we were older, we understood why Grandmother got so upset.

Grandpa King also had an orchard. Grandma dried sour cherries and apples. She also dried orange peel and ate it. Because money was too scarce, we seldom had an orange at that time, except at Christmastime. Instead, we ate apples.

MY MOTHER AND AUNT MATTIE

I remember well my mother's two sisters who lived in Big Valley in the Belleville area. Mary was married to Jonas Yoder who in later years moved to Lancaster County at Compass. I don't remember this move. Aunt Mattie married Noah Hostettler on July 28, 1891. My mother seldom saw her sisters more then twice a year. The last time Aunt Lizzie visited before my mother's death was on August 24, 1923. Mother went to Grandad's to bid good-bye to Aunt Mattie. They loved each other so much and knew that they wouldn't meet again soon. They ran across the road three times to kiss each other good-bye. That was the last time they saw each other on this earth.

Grandmother King called out to them, "Now girls, that's enough," and they parted. Mother looked back waving on her way home.

VISITING AUNT MATTIE

In 1918, David F. Fisher went with Dad to Mifflin County in Belleville to visit. I went along. My baby sister Mary went along. David Fisher's Anna was also a baby and went along. I don't remember how many days we were there, perhaps a week or so. I was only five years old at the time. I often fell asleep on David Fisher's lap in the evenings. I got homesick missing my sisters back home and took sick and vomited. Aunt Mattie gave me some horse trough water to drink to cure my homesickness. Grandma believed that was a remedy for homesickness.

DAD

We traveled by train back then. There were no vans, but even if there were we wouldn't have thought of going that way because the Amish were seldom seen in cars in those days.

Dr. Mylin took Dad to the hospital in October 1923 after he was kicked in the abdomen by a horse. They sped to the hospital at 40 miles an hour which was very fast at that time. Dad had his bowels torn and was not expected to pull through. He was hospitalized for weeks and had a special nurse around the clock for $3.00 a day. I remember my mother crying a lot back then. Dad couldn't do work for the entire winter and when the spring came he sweated so much that he caught pneumonia.

Dad bought steers to feed and sell them when they were fat. When they were sold we drove them to Leaman Place at the railroad station where they were put on cattle cars and sent out west. It was exciting. In some places there were no fences, and the girls were afraid they'd go wild at times, as they ran and jumped while on the road.

There were no cattle trucks at that time. I remember

watching cattle in the fields after wheat harvesting each evening until we were good and tired of it.

CHRISTMAS

At Christmas, I remember him (Dad) giving me a fruit dish with one orange in it, which happened a couple of times. There weren't many toys back then. We played with spools and blocks. Spools were our animals. Often we cut pictures out of Sears Roebuck and Montgomery Ward's catalogs.

Sometimes when mother was washing she would make a "house" for us with four chairs. She fastened a blanket at the corners of the chairs. That was great fun. Sometimes we had church there in our tent.

DID WITH WHAT WE HAD

When Grandpa's sister got married, they started farming. Within a few days their, food supplies got low, so she gave her new husband a list to go to the grocery store. He looked at it for awhile, then he said, "Write down what we need."

In those days you weighed your own sugar, flour, salt, etc., with a little scoop, then put it in a paper bag. They had no plastic bags. Their store bill was a small amount. When their first baby arrived they just used their wash basket for their crib.

Over that time, there was a sale. When the sale was almost over the man pulled his watch out of his pocket and sold it also to help pay this department. The person that bought it gave it back to him the next day after the sale. Will history repeat itself someday again?

Sayings from Grandma's Scrapbooks

A HORSE'S PRAYER

Up hill wear me, Down hill spare me, On the level let me trot, In the stable forget me not.

Most folks look forward to happiness—forgetting that now is the future they used to look forward to. Life is what happens to you while you are making other plans. Life is like a bridge. Cross over it. But don't establish yourself upon it. A kindly word that falls today, may bear its fruits tomorrow. A helpful friend in time of need is as valuable as a support to a leaning wall. Acts of love and kindness never die, but in the lives of others multiply.

SCENIC ROAD

Find that with the passing years. My pace is getting a little slow. I may not go far or fast, but I see more along the road.

YOU CANNOT COUNT A TRILLION

It is impossible to count a trillion. H. Cod. Adams counted continuously from his creation to the present day. He would not have reached that number, for it would take him over 9,512 years. At the rate of 200 a minute, there could be counted 12,000 an hour, 288,000 a day, and 105,120,000 a year.

SELF DESTRUCT

There was an old man of Blackhealth. He sat on a set of fake teeth. He cried with a start. Oh Lord, bless my heart. I've bitten myself underneath.

A man is a funny creature. He can't wait on his wife for ten minutes. But he can stand motionless for hours waiting on a fish.

The man who does things makes many mistakes, but he never makes the biggest mistake of all—doing nothing.

A man must learn to know himself first—before a neighborhood or church can be any value to him.

AN OLDER PERSON

An older person with their grandchild can go driving down the road. The older person starts talking, saying this person lived here and that person lived there. The grandchild doesn't know of them or ever heard of such a person.